D1143283

5148

# NATURAL WORLD

# BLACK RHINO

## HABITATS • LIFE CYCLES • FOOD CHAINS • THREATS

## Malcolm Penny

HODDER
*Wayland*

an imprint of Hodder
Children's Books

**WWF**®

## Produced in Association with WWF-UK

# NATURAL WORLD

Black Rhino • Chimpanzee • Crocodile • Dolphin • Elephant •
Giant Panda • Giraffe • Golden Eagle • Great White Shark •
Grizzly Bear • Hippopotamus • Killer Whale • Leopard •
Lion • Orangutan • Penguin • Polar Bear • Tiger

Produced for Hodder Wayland by
Roger Coote Publishing
Gissing's Farm, Fressingfield
Suffolk IP21 5SH, UK

WWF is a registered charity no. 1081247
WWF-UK, Panda House, Weyside Park
Godalming, Surrey GU7 1XR

**Cover:** A black rhinoceros in northern Kenya.
**Title page:** A black rhinoceros in the Lewa Downs Game Reserve, Kenya.
**Contents page:** The black rhino's horns are fearsome weapons.
**Index page:** Two black rhinos rub noses in Zimbabwe.

Text copyright © 2001 Hodder Wayland
Volume copyright © 2001 Hodder Wayland

Editor: Polly Goodman
Series editor: Victoria Brooker
Designer: Sarah Crouch

Published in Great Britain in 2001 by Hodder Wayland,
an imprint of Hodder Children's Books

**British Library Cataloguing in Publication Data**
Penny, Malcolm
    Black rhino. - (Natural world)
    1. Black rhinoceros - Juvenile literature
    I. Title
    599.6'68

ISBN 0 7502 3404 0

Printed and bound in G. Canale & C.Sp.A., Turin, Italy

Hodder Children's Books
A division of Hodder Headline Limited
338 Euston Road, London NW1 3BH

**Picture acknowledgements**
*Ardea* 7 Adrian Warren, 9 Jean-Paul Ferrero, 11, 13
Clem Haagner, 19 M.Watson, 25 Alan Weaving, 33,
35 Ferrero-Labat, 38 Piers Cavendish, 45 (top)
Clem Haagner, 45 (centre) Ferrero-Labat; *Bruce
Coleman* 6, 8, 12, 24 Christer Fredriksson, 32 M.P.L.
Fogden, 45 (bottom); *Corbis* 41 Anthony
Bannister/Gallo Images; *Digital Vision* 8, 16, 36;
*FLPA* 14 David Hosking, 21 T.Whittaker, 22 David
Hosking, 26 Philip Perry, 27 David Hosking, 37
L.Batten, 39 David Hosking, 44 (middle) David
Hosking; *Getty Images* 3 Theo Allofs, 15 Nicholas
Parfitt, 34 Tim Davis, 44 (bottom) Nicholas Parfitt,
48 Ian Murphy; *NHPA* 1 Kevin Schafer, 20 Stephen
Krasemann, 23 Derek Balfour, 28 Martin Harvey,
29 T.Kitchin & V.Hurst, 42 Martin Harvey, 43 Ken
Griffiths; *Oxford Scientific Films Cover* Steve Turner,
10 Miriam Austerman, 17 Steve Turner, 30 John
Downer, 31 Steve Turner, 44 (top) Miriam
Austerman. Map on page 4 by Victoria Webb.
All other artworks by Michael Posen.

# Contents

# Meet the Black Rhino

The black rhinoceros lives in Africa, south of the Sahara Desert. The name 'rhinoceros' comes from two Greek words and means 'nose-horned', from the horns on the rhino's nose.

The black rhino is one of the most endangered large animals in Africa. Over the last thirty years, its numbers have dropped by over 62,000 due to poachers killing rhinos for their horns. Today there are less than 2,300 still alive and the black rhino is in danger of becoming extinct.

▼ The red shading on this map shows where black rhinos live in Africa today. The smaller map shows Africa's position in the world.

**AFRICA**

**Skin**
The black rhino isn't black at all, but grey. Its thick, hairless skin protects it from thorns, but it is sensitive to sunburn.

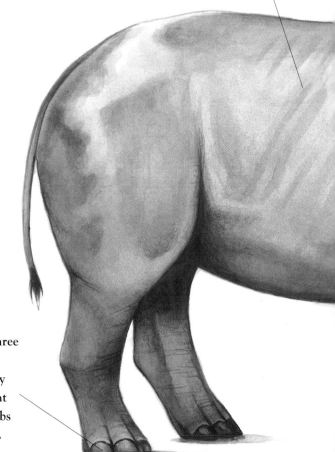

**Feet**
All rhinos have three toes, with thick padded soles. They produce a footprint like the ace of clubs in a pack of cards.

# BLACK RHINO FACTS

The black rhino's scientific name is *Diceros bicornis*, which means 'two horned'. The word *diceros* comes from the Greek word *di* meaning 'two' and *ceros* meaning 'horn'.

•

Male rhinos are known as bulls, and females as cows. Young rhinos are called calves.

•

Adults grow up to 3.8 metres from nose to tail, and 1.8 metres tall at the shoulder. They weigh up to 1,400 kilograms.

**Ears**
The rhino's ears are large and move around quickly and easily. They help it find out where strange sounds are coming from.

**Horns**
Black rhinos have two horns, which grow throughout their lives. The horns are made of keratin fibres, which human hair and nails are also made of. The keratin is matted together so that it is light, but hard and sharp. The front horn of an adult rhino is 50–135 centimetres long.

**Nose**
A rhino has a very good sense of smell, to make up for its poor long-distance eyesight.

**Eyes**
Black rhinos are short-sighted, which means they cannot see long-distance objects very well. However, they can see close-up objects quite well.

**Mouth**
The black rhino's top lip is pointed and able to grasp twigs and leaves, its main diet. This type of lip is called a prehensile lip. The teeth are strong and flat on top, to grind up food.

## Habitat

Black rhinos live in woodland savannah, where there are plenty of trees and bushes. They feed on twigs and leaves from the bushes. The rhino's thick skin and sturdy build help it push through areas of dense thorn bush, where other animals find it hard to travel.

▼ The thick bushes of the Serengeti Plains in Tanzania provide an ideal habitat for rhinos.

▲ Black rhino skin is thick and tough, but sensitive to touch – and to sunburn.

Rhinos need to be able to find water every day, even in the dry season, so they are never more than 5 kilometres from a waterhole. At one time, black rhinos lived all over Africa except in parts of East Africa, where it is too dry and in the western forests, where it is too hot and damp. Today they have become very rare in most parts of Africa because of poaching and the loss of their habitat.

Adult males live mainly alone, while females live with their most recent young, and sometimes an elder daughter. Young rhinos that have left their mothers team up with at least one other young rhino in small groups of up to five.

## Relatives

Modern rhinos are the last of a very ancient line of animals, which appeared about 50 million years ago. There used to be many different species, including some in North America, but most have now become extinct.

Today there are only five species of rhinoceros. The black rhino and its closest relative the white rhino live in Africa. The other three species live in Asia. Some species have two horns, while others have only one.

▲ The white rhino, with its square lips, is adapted to feed on short grass, which the black rhino cannot eat.

### RHINO ANCESTORS

The rhino's distant ancestors were enormous, and included the largest land mammal that ever lived. One, called *Indricotherium*, lived on the plains of Mongolia. It stood 6 metres tall at the shoulder and was 7 metres long. It had no horns, but two sharp tusks in its lower jaw. It became extinct 10 million years ago.

## WHAT'S THE DIFFERENCE?

| BLACK RHINOS | WHITE RHINOS |
| --- | --- |
| Pointed upper lip | Square lips |
| Solitary animals | Sociable animals |
| Smaller | Bigger |
| More aggressive | More docile |
| Good swimmers | Poor swimmers |

White rhinos live out in the open savannah, grazing on grass. They are much larger than black rhinos. After the elephant, white rhinos are the largest land mammals. Both black and white rhinos can live side by side in southern Africa because they eat different food.

The Indian, or greater one-horned rhinoceros, lives in India and Nepal. It only has one horn. The very rare Javan (or lesser one-horned) rhino and Sumatran rhinos live in Southeast Asia.

▼ The Sumatran, or hairy rhino, is probably the most endangered rhino species. Numbers have dropped by over half in the last ten years. Less than 300 survive in Southeast Asia.

# A Black Rhino is Born

About fifteen months (446–548 days) after she mated, a black rhino cow is ready to give birth. It is very rare for humans to see a rhino being born in the wild, and other rhinos probably never see it either. The heavily pregnant cow hides herself away in thick bush. She avoids all other rhinos, especially males, which might injure her new calf.

▲ A black rhino mother suckles her calf in the Los Angeles Zoo, USA. Rhinos are rarely seen being born in the wild.

The mother rhino gives birth standing up. The single, new-born calf weighs between 25 and 40 kilograms and can walk within 10 minutes of being born. The mother will suckle her calf within its first three hours. It will stay close to her side wherever she goes for safety.

▼ A black rhino mother can be very aggressive when she has a calf to defend.

## BLACK RHINO CALVES

A new-born calf can be 60 centimetres tall and weigh up to 40 kilograms. A black rhino calf weighs only about 4 per cent of its mother's weight when it is born, the same as an African elephant. In comparison, humans weigh between 6 and 8 per cent of their mother's weight.

## Early days

The mother rhino and her new calf stay away from other rhinos for two weeks, hidden deep in the bush. The calf can see well and has very sharp hearing, even at this early age. Its mother leads the way through the bush, pushing aside the sharp thorns to make a path for her calf. She must be very alert, in case they meet a bull. Bulls have been known to injure young calves by trampling on them, although no one knows why they do this.

▶ With their stamina and teamwork, spotted hyenas are very efficient predators on the African savannah.

▼ A black rhino's charge can be very dangerous. They have been known to kill people.

Lions and hyenas are also a threat to young rhino calves. If a bull, lion or hyena approaches, the mother rhino will stand sideways between her calf and the approaching danger. If the enemy does not move away, the mother will charge, using upward thrusts of her sharp front horn. Usually a short charge, with much huffing and puffing, is enough to send the enemy away. Rhinos can kill people in this way, if the rhino is taken by surprise in the bush.

## CALF DEATHS

About one in every six black rhino calves die in their first two years of life. The main cause of death is attack by spotted hyenas, which can team up to outwit mother rhinos.

▲ Black rhino calves follow behind their mother, even in open countryside.

## WHO GOES FIRST?

Black rhino calves always follow their mother, whereas white rhino calves walk in front. Both species of calves can see better than the adult rhino, so it makes sense for the calf to lead the way. But the bush in the black rhino's habitat is too thick for the calf to push through, so the mother goes first, to save her calf from being scratched by the thorns.

## Calf life

The calf grows quickly on its mother's rich milk. She has two teats between her hind legs, and she suckles her calf standing up. This is the only time in her life when the cow does not wallow in cooling mud every day, probably to make sure that her teats are clean and safe for the calf to drink from.

The calf will try its first solid food before it is a few months old, but it will continue sucking its mother's milk until it reaches the age of two years. Sometimes a calf will feed from its mother when it is so big that it has to lie down to get its head underneath her. The calf explores its surroundings with great curiosity and energy, but never moves more than a few metres from its mother.

▼ A two-year-old black rhino calf struggles to drink its mother's milk.

# Learning to Survive

As the rhino calf grows bigger, it travels round with its mother to good feeding places and waterholes. There it will meet other black rhino calves and often play with them, perhaps picking up sticks or pretending to fight. The calf will never know its father. He left as soon as he had made its mother pregnant. The young rhino completely depends on its mother for protection as well as for guidance.

▼ Zebras share the open parts of the rhino's habitat, but rarely go into the thick bush.

▲ A mother and her calf of three months in a bush clearing.

## Neighbours

The young calf will also meet the other animals that share its bush habitat. There are giraffes, which browse high above the rhino's head, and small, secretive antelope such as dik-dik, which use the thick undergrowth to hide from their enemies.

### RHINO TRACKS

Rhino tracks are about 30 centimetres deep and 50 centimetres wide, in a tunnel about 180 centimetres high. The tracks are used as highways by many other animals.

17

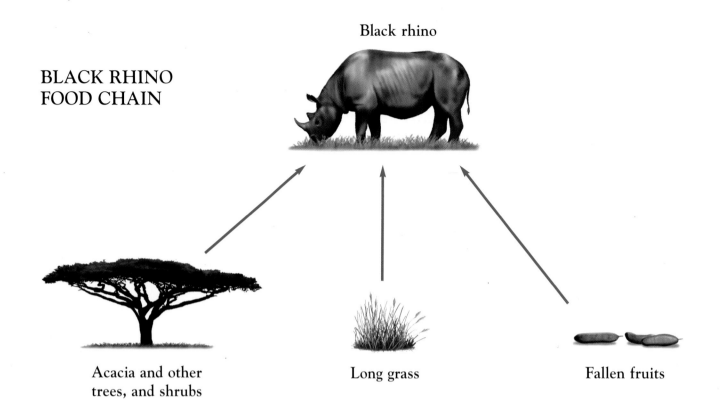

BLACK RHINO
FOOD CHAIN

Black rhino

Acacia and other
trees, and shrubs

Long grass

Fallen fruits

## Food

By the time it is two years old, the rhino calf stops feeding on its mother's milk and eats the same food as adults. Black rhinos eat leaves and twigs from trees and bushes, even those of the thorniest acacia bushes. This type of feeding is called browsing. The rhinos use their horns to pull branches within reach, and they use their prehensile upper lip to grip and twist twigs until they break. They can also use their lip to pull up clumps of long grass or clover, twisting it into bundles when other food is scarce, or to pick up fallen fruits.

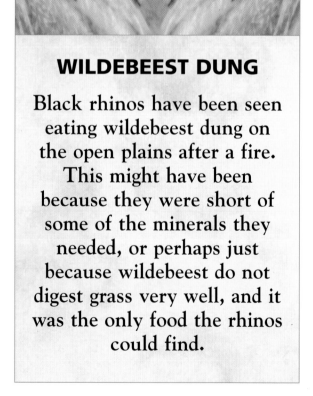

### WILDEBEEST DUNG

Black rhinos have been seen eating wildebeest dung on the open plains after a fire. This might have been because they were short of some of the minerals they needed, or perhaps just because wildebeest do not digest grass very well, and it was the only food the rhinos could find.

The black rhino's food chain is very simple. It consists of all the plants they can eat. Since they have no natural predators, adult black rhinos are at the top of their own food chain.

▼ Any form of bush or shrub that it can reach is food to a black rhino.

## Drinking

Water is very important for black rhinos. In the worst of the dry season, when it does not rain for several months, they can survive without water for three or four days. But rhinos really need water every day. This is why they are almost always found within 5 kilometres of permanent water, usually a waterhole rather than a river.

In very dry conditions, when the waterholes are empty and even the rivers have run dry, rhinos dig in the sandy river beds to find water.

◀ Rhinos are avoided by other animals at waterholes, though they seldom cause any trouble except to other rhinos.

▼ A mother rhino and her three-month-old calf cool their bodies with damp mud.

## Wallowing

Rhinos need water for wallowing, as well as drinking. The black rhino is unable to sweat, so it overheats easily. It is also hairless, so its skin is sensitive to sunburn. Lying and rolling in water or wet mud helps keep the rhino's skin in good condition and stops it overheating. When the mud dries, it also protects the rhino against flies and other blood-sucking parasites. It can also act as a type of sunblock.

## Rolling

A young rhino calf will be taken by its mother to a wallowing place very early in its life, although it will stay away from the mud until it is big enough to be able to climb out again safely.

When the calf leaves the wallow, the mother rolls energetically in dust or ash to dry the mud. Her youngster imitates her. At first this is just for fun, but for the rest of its life, rolling in the dust will help to keep the rhino's skin in good condition.

▼ Two black rhinos 'dust' themselves by rolling in the dust in Tanzania.

▶ A black rhino with an infected sore behind its shoulder.

## Rubbing

Rubbing is also important to rhinos, to get rid of irritating skin parasites that suck their blood. Favourite rubbing posts, rocks or tree stumps have become polished by generations of rhinos scrubbing their skin against them.

There is just one place that all this rolling and rubbing cannot reach, and that is behind the elbows of the front legs. Most black rhinos have a sore place there, where parasites cannot be removed.

## Helpers

Black rhinos are infested with over twenty species of skin parasites, such as ticks and worms, which bite their skin and suck their blood. But several animals help the rhinos by removing and eating the ticks.

The main helper is a small bird called an ox-pecker. It climbs all over large mammals, picking the ticks from their skin, even from sensitive places like ears and nostrils. The animals put up with the birds' scratchy feet for the sake of having their parasites removed.

▲ Terrapins and their young bask in the sunshine by a waterhole.

◄ When they feed on antelope, ox-peckers take a little fur to line their nests. All they get from rhinos, which are hairless, is the chance to eat ticks.

More unexpected is a small terrapin, which visits waterholes where rhinos are wallowing. It pulls out ticks from a rhino's skin underwater. As many as six rhinos have been seen lying together in a wallow while terrapins removed their ticks.

The sores behind a rhino's front legs are infested by a small worm. The worm's eggs are carried by a fly, which breeds in the rhino's dung piles. The size of the dung piles is reduced by scarab, or dung beetles, which carry the dung away to bury it and lay their eggs in it. Without the work of the dung beetles, Africa would be metres deep in animal dung.

# Adult Life

When its mother is expecting a new calf, young male rhinos are driven away. By this time they are at least two, sometimes as old as five years. Female calves often stay with their mother, even after a new calf is born.

After leaving its mother, the young male rhino will often meet other males in the bush, and live with them in a group. Sometimes they team up with a mother whose calf has died, until she becomes pregnant again. The groups of young males often stay together until they are fully grown.

## HOME RANGES

The home ranges of rhino bulls can be up to 4 square kilometres. Cows wander over a much bigger home range, depending on how much food there is. In good feeding country, a cow's home range might be only 3 square kilometres, but if food is scarce, it might cover 90 square kilometres. Cows wander across the home ranges of bulls. There is usually under one rhino in every square kilometre of land.

A male black rhino spraying his territory. Males recognize the scent of other males' urine, so spraying trees and bushes leaves a clear sign of who owns a territory.

## Home ranges

Rhinos are fully grown at about seven years old. At this age, male rhinos leave any group they are part of and find their own home range, or territory. This is an area surrounding a waterhole, never more than 5 kilometres away. The young rhino clearly marks the borders of his home range with dung piles and sprays them with urine to scent them. However, he does not carefully patrol the borders, so different home ranges often overlap.

◄ A black rhino wanders through its territory in the Masai Mara National Park, in Kenya. Where the grass is long enough, rhinos can pull it up in bunches.

## Clans

Rhino bulls may live on their own, but they will be familiar with any neighbouring rhinos. Without actually being friendly to other male rhinos, they tolerate them, forming a local group called a clan, which usually has about five members. The members of a clan may tolerate each other, but they attack strangers.

## Fighting

Black rhinos rarely fight amongst themselves, possibly because they are armed with such fearsome weapons. The danger of being wounded is too great. In this they are different from white rhinos, which fight fiercely, though usually without serious injuries.

Most of the time, black rhinos try to avoid each other, turning aside when they come across the scent trails of other rhinos in the bush. These trails are scented with flakes of skin and dung scraped off rhino skin by thorns. They also carry the scent of dung from rhinos' feet, since rhinos scrape dung piles with their feet after they have added to them.

▲ Two male rhinos fighting. When they do occur, fights can be serious, often with both parties being hurt.

Male and female rhinos sometimes quarrel during the breeding season, and males challenge other males on the rare occasions when they meet at a disputed border. However, instead of fighting, black rhinos make short charges towards each other, usually stopping at least 6 metres away. Occasionally, they push and wrestle with their horns. This soon tells the lighter animal that it does not have a chance of winning, so it retreats.

▼ A junior male black rhino avoids conflict with a bigger bull by lying down to show that he has no intention of fighting.

## Communicating

Black rhinos use a wide range of sounds to communicate with each other. An adult approaching a waterhole gives a regular puffing sound so that any others know it is coming. The others can then decide whether to let it join them, or challenge it and drive it away. Usually their response is friendly. Waterholes seem to be neutral places, where fighting is rare.

A bull challenging another bull makes loud snorts, pawing the ground to express its anger and to warn its opponent that there will be a fight if it doesn't retreat. Mothers and calves squeal and grunt to each other, although since they can see each other most of the time it is hard to know why they need to do this.

▶ Soft squeals and grunts seem to reassure both mother and calf that the other hasn't strayed far away, even though they might only be separated by thick bush.

▼ Gatherings of adult black rhinos are rare. They are usually seen only at waterholes.

## CALF SQUEALS

If a black rhino bull hears a calf squealing, it will come from as far as a kilometre away to investigate. This might be because where there is a calf, there will be a female (its mother), and bulls are always looking for females to mate with. However, when the bull arrives, it will usually be driven away by the mother if her calf is still small.

# Breeding Time

Black rhinos mate at any time of the year, although there is a peak at the end of the rainy seasons. In Kenya there are two rainy seasons: the 'long' rains are between March and May, and the shorter rains are in October.

Bachelor bulls, who have not found a mate, remain in their clans waiting for a female to pass through their home range. If he is very lucky, one of them will meet a cow who does not reject him, allowing him to come close enough to begin courting her. However, this is very rare. Females with small young usually drive off any male that comes close to them.

▼ Even when he is fully grown, at nearly ten years old, a young bull will have trouble finding a mate.

## BREEDING AGE

Rhino cows can breed from the age of five to seven years, before they are fully grown. Bulls have to wait until they are at least seven, usually ten years old, when they will be big enough to dominate other, older bulls.

▼ A black rhino bull has found a cow in season, with a nineteen-month-old calf. If she accepts the bull as a mate, she will drive her calf away before the next one is born.

## HOW MANY CALVES?

On average, rhino cows give birth to a single calf every two-and-a-half to four years. A female may produce up to fourteen calves during her lifetime, but eight or nine is the average.

▼ Black rhinos grunt and puff at each other when they meet, but they very rarely fight.

## Courtship and mating

When a bull approaches her, a black rhino cow usually becomes very aggressive, charging and ploughing the ground with her horn to drive him away from her calf. The male may respond by brushing his horn on the ground, and charging bushes, to show the female what he could do to her if he dared! This often drives her into an even greater temper, but eventually, if she is receptive, she calms down.

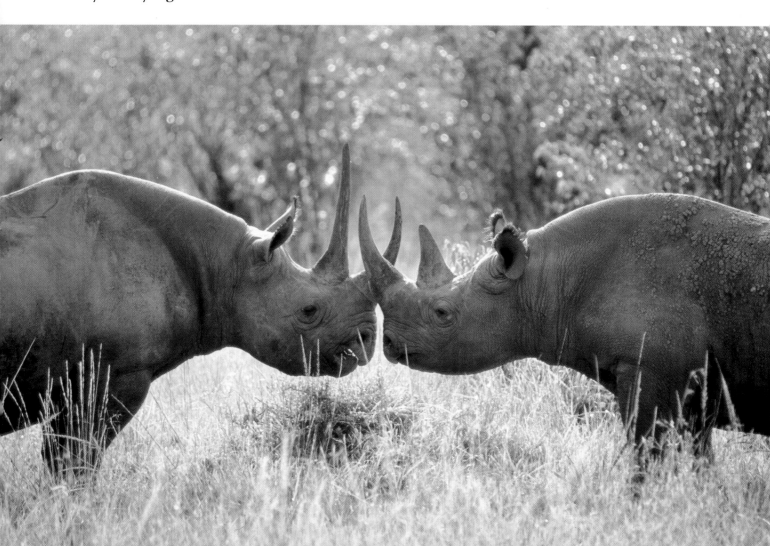

▲ The cow needs to brace herself to take the great weight of a mating bull for half an hour at a time.

Once he has been accepted as a mate, a black rhino bull is surprisingly gentle when he is courting a female. Because he is so heavy, he has to prepare the female to support his weight before he mounts her. He does this by laying his heavy head across her back, causing her to brace her legs. Mating lasts for 20 to 35 minutes and takes place several times a day, before the female finally wanders away.

# Threats

Once it is fully grown, the black rhino has few natural predators. Older rhinos, especially if they are sick or injured, are sometimes taken by lions. A lion can sometimes manage to bite the rhino's throat and chest, where its skin is thinner, and wrestle it to the ground to make a kill. However, a healthy adult rhino is more likely to kill a lion than be killed by it.

The main enemies of black rhinos are humans. When new farmland is created, one of the first jobs is to remove dangerous animals, and black rhinos are an early target. But most rhinos are killed by poachers for their horns.

▲ A lioness on the lookout for prey.

## Poaching

Rhino horns are worth a lot of money in the Far East and in some Arab countries, and thousands of rhinos have been killed by poachers over the last thirty years.

▼ This rhino has been killed by poachers. They removed both of its horns.

## PEST CONTROL

The number of ox-peckers has been reduced in southern Africa by the use of pesticides on farm animals, especially in Zambia. The birds die from eating poisoned ticks on domestic cattle. This means there are fewer ox-peckers to clean ticks from wildlife, including rhinos. People are now trying to reintroduce ox-peckers in areas where the use of pesticides has been reduced.

## How rhino horn is used

In traditional Chinese medicine, ground-up rhino horn is used to cure a wide range of diseases, from fevers to bowel disorders, and in some places it is regarded as an aphrodisiac.

▼ This stall in Burma is selling rhino horns and parts of other animals, including snake and monkey skins.

**RHINO NUMBERS**

In 1970, there were about 65,000 black rhinos in Africa. Today, numbers have fallen to less than 2,300.

In Arab countries, rhino horn is used to make the handle of a traditional ceremonial dagger, called a jambia, which is given to each boy when he becomes a man. A rhino-horn dagger costs more than one made from gold. Both these markets offer poachers enormous sums of money for rhino horns, which makes poaching very difficult to stop.

▲ The jambia, or ceremonial dagger, is worn by many men in Yemen. Those with handles made from rhino horn are considered the most valuable.

## Conserving black rhinos

Since rhino horn is so valuable, many countries have tried to stop poachers by force. These attempts were unsuccessful at first. In the 1980s, poachers arriving in Zimbabwe from Zambia were met by the army, and many poachers and some soldiers were killed in the resulting shoot-outs. Finally, the surviving rhinos were moved south, away from the border, to be protected in nature reserves.

Almost all wild rhinos have now been captured and put in nature reserves, where teams of rangers watch over them. In some places, high electric fences surround the reserves and it has been proved that rhinos can breed well where their habitat is suitable.

▲ An armed anti-poaching guard in the Imire Game Reserve, in Zimbabwe. Fencing and guards are expensive, but they have been successful in protecting the last remaining rhinos.

▶ Rhinos being dehorned by wildlife officials.

Anti-poaching work is still an important part of rhino conservation. However, there are also efforts to reduce the value of the rhino horn by encouraging people not to buy it. There has been some progress in Arab countries such as Yemen, where daggers made from rhino horn are no longer the status symbol they once were, but the Chinese medicine market is still flourishing.

## DEHORNING

An early attempt to stop poaching was to remove the horns of living rhinos using saws. Later, rangers found that poachers would kill a rhino even for the small new horn as it grew back. They were also afraid that dehorning would spoil the rhinos' territorial and courtship displays, so dehorning is not practised any more.

## Tourism

Black rhinos, along with many other large animals, are a valuable tourist attraction. For many African countries, tourism is an important source of income. If rhinos and other large animals in the wildlife reserves become too rare, the number of tourists will fall, and the income will dry up.

▲ An African safari is among the most popular overseas holidays, and a good source of income for the host countries.

## Breeding black rhinos

The first black rhino was born in captivity in Chicago Zoo in 1941. Since then they have been bred successfully and regularly in zoos.

▶ Black rhinos breed well in captivity, but none have ever been released into the wild from a zoo.

42

## LIFE EXPECTANCY

In zoos, black rhinos have lived for more than forty years. Their life expectancy in the wild is not known for certain, but two females studied in Amboseli National Park, Kenya, in 1966, were between thirty-two and forty years old. Their natural life span was never discovered, however, because they were both speared by poachers in 1967.

Sanctuaries for black rhinos have been established in several countries, especially in Zimbabwe and Kenya, where they have been bred in semi-captivity. But the main aim is to persuade them to breed successfully in the wild. In Natal, South Africa, scientists discovered that black rhinos breed most successfully in large game reserves if there are not too many rhinos crowded together. Since then, the population in southern Africa has risen steadily, so that there, at least, the black rhino should be safe for many years.

# Black Rhino Life Cycle

 1 > Fifteen or sixteen months after mating, the rhino cow gives birth to a single calf, hidden in thick bush.

2  The young calf can walk within ten minutes of being born and feeds from its mother within three hours.

 3 > At about two weeks old, the calf begins to mix with other calves. At one-and-a-half years it tries its first solid food. By two years, the calf stops drinking its mother's milk and now feeds just on leaves and twigs.

4 Between two and five years old, male calves are driven away by their mothers and join other males. Females stay with their mother until they are ready to breed.

5 Females first start to breed from the age of five years. Males must wait until they are about ten.

6 At seven years old the rhino is fully grown. Rhinos have been known to live to over forty years old.

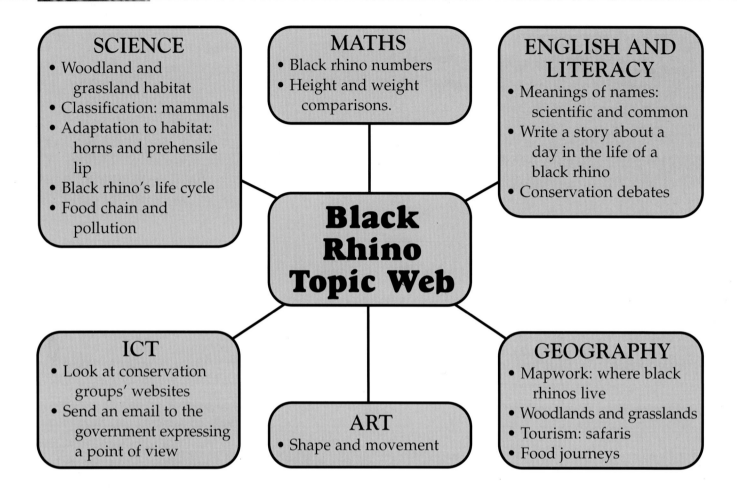

## Black Rhino Topic Web

**SCIENCE**
- Woodland and grassland habitat
- Classification: mammals
- Adaptation to habitat: horns and prehensile lip
- Black rhino's life cycle
- Food chain and pollution

**MATHS**
- Black rhino numbers
- Height and weight comparisons.

**ENGLISH AND LITERACY**
- Meanings of names: scientific and common
- Write a story about a day in the life of a black rhino
- Conservation debates

**ICT**
- Look at conservation groups' websites
- Send an email to the government expressing a point of view

**ART**
- Shape and movement

**GEOGRAPHY**
- Mapwork: where black rhinos live
- Woodlands and grasslands
- Tourism: safaris
- Food journeys

# Extension Activities

**English**
- Debate whether black rhinos should be kept in zoos.
- Find and list collective names for groups of animals, or terms for their young e.g. calf, cub, chick.

**Geography**
- Trace a world map from an atlas. Show the location of Africa and the Sahara Desert.
- Draw a black rhino distribution map.

**Maths**
- Use the black rhino's head as a model to develop work on symmetry.

**Art**
- Make a savannah frieze, with black rhinos and other animals that share their habitat.

**Science**
- Make a display showing the ways in which black rhinos are adapted to their habitat.

# Glossary

**Aphrodisiac** A medicine or food that is supposed to make men and women more attractive to each other. Western doctors say that this is a myth.

**Browse** Eat twigs and leaves from bushes and trees.

**Bush** Wooded country away from agriculture and civilization.

**Dry season** The period between rainy seasons.

**Endangered** A species that is in danger of extinction.

**Extinct** No longer existing.

**Habitat** The natural home for an animal or plant.

**Home range** The area defended by an animal in which it finds food and water.

**Poaching** Killing animals that are protected by law.

**Prehensile** Able to grasp objects.

**Savannah** Open grassland with clumps of trees.

**Suckles** A female animal suckles her young by feeding it milk through her teats.

**Ticks** Insect parasites that suck blood by piercing the skin.

**Wallowing** Lying and rolling in water or mud.

**Waterhole** A depression in the ground filled with water from a spring.

# Further Information

## Organizations to Contact

Care for the Wild International
1 Ashfolds, Horsham Road,
Rusper, West Sussex
RH12 4QX
Tel: 01293 871596
Website:
www.careforthewild.org.uk

WWF-UK
Panda House, Weyside Park
Godalming, Surrey GU7 1XR
Tel: 01483 426444
Website: www.wwf-uk.org

## Websites

International Rhino
Foundation
www.rhinos-irf.org
Information about the current status and threats to each of the five species of rhino.

The Sebakwe Black
Rhino Trust
www.blackrhino.org

Nature Wildlife Photo Gallery
www.nature-wildlife.com

## Books to Read

*The Atlas of Endangered Animals* by Steve Pollock (Belitha Press, 1994)

*Nature Encyclopedia* (Dorling Kindersley, 1998)

*Natural World: Hippopotamus* by Michael Leach (Hodder Wayland, 2000)

*What is a Mammal* by Robert Snedden (Belitha Press, 1997)

47

# Index

Page numbers in **bold** refer to photographs or illustrations.